United States Presidents

William H. Harrison

Paul Joseph
ABDO Publishing Company

visit us at
www.abdopub.com

Published by Abdo Publishing Company 4940 Viking Drive, Edina, Minnesota 55435.
Copyright © 1999 by Abdo Consulting Group, Inc. International copyrights reserved in
all countries. No part of this book may be reproduced in any form without written
permission from the publisher.

Printed in the United States.

Cover and Interior Photo credits: AP/Wide World, Archive, Corbis-Bettmann

Contributing editors: Robert Italia, Tamara L. Britton, K. M. Brielmaier
Book design/maps: Patrick Laurel

Library of Congress Cataloging-in-Publication Data

Joseph, Paul, 1970-
    William H. Harrison / Paul Joseph.
        p. cm. -- (United States presidents)
    Includes index.
    Summary: A biography of the president who served the shortest term, dying
after being in office only thirty-one days.
    ISBN 1-57765-232-0
    1. Harrison, William Henry, 1773-1841--Juvenile literature. 2. Presidents--
United States--Biography--Juvenile literature. [1. Harrison, William Henry,
1773-1841. 2. Presidents.] I. Title. II. Series: United States presidents (Edina,
Minn.)
E392.J67   1999
973.5'8'092--dc21
    [B]   98-5882
                                                                    CIP
                                                                     AC

Contents

SOUTHWESTERN   3/00 13 95

William H. Harrison

William Henry Harrison spent the shortest time in office of any U.S. president. Harrison became sick at his **inauguration**. He died 31 days later. All he did was name his **cabinet**.

When he was 18 years old, Harrison joined the military. He was a **captain** when he left the army. Then he worked in farming and business. During the **War of 1812**, Harrison joined the army again. He became a **major general**. After the war, he ran for the U.S. Senate and won.

At 68 years old, Harrison was the oldest person to become president. Harrison was also the first president to die in office. As a military leader, he played an important role in American history.

William Henry
Harrison

William H. Harrison (1773-1841)
Ninth President

BORN:	February 9, 1773
PLACE OF BIRTH:	Charles City County, Virginia
ANCESTRY:	English
FATHER:	Benjamin Harrison (1726-1791)
MOTHER:	Elizabeth Bassett Harrison (1730-1792)
WIFE:	Anna Tuthill Symmes (1775-1864)
CHILDREN:	Ten: 6 boys, 4 girls
EDUCATION:	Private tutoring; attended Hampden-Sydney College
RELIGION:	Episcopalian
OCCUPATION:	Soldier
MILITARY SERVICE:	U.S. Army (1791-1798), rose from ensign to captain; as governor of Indiana Territory, fought Shawnee at Tippecanoe (1811); commissioned major general of Kentucky Militia (1812); U.S. Army (1812-1814), rose from brigadier general to major general in command of the Northwest Territory
POLITICAL PARTY:	Whig

OFFICES HELD:	Secretary of Northwest Territory; member of U.S. House of Representatives; governor of Indiana Territory and superintendent of Indian Affairs; Ohio state senator; U.S. senator; minister to Colombia
AGE AT INAUGURATION:	68
YEARS SERVED:	31 days
VICE PRESIDENT:	John Tyler
DIED:	April 4, 1841, Washington, D.C., age 68
CAUSE OF DEATH:	Pneumonia

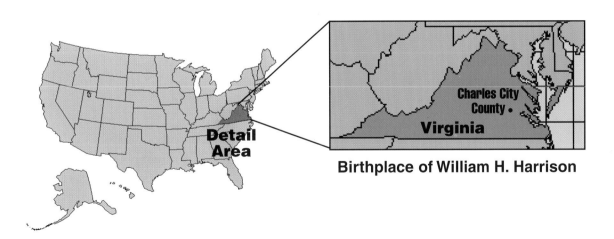

Birthplace of William H. Harrison

Early Years

William Harrison was born on February 9, 1773, in Charles City County, Virginia. Virginia was a British colony.

William was the third son of Benjamin and Elizabeth Harrison. The Harrisons were wealthy and well known. They lived on a **plantation** on the James River.

William's father, Benjamin, was the governor of Virginia. Benjamin was called "the Signer." He had signed the **Declaration of Independence**.

William studied at home until 1787. Then he went to Hampden-Sydney College in Virginia. In 1790, he decided to become a doctor. He left college and moved to Philadelphia. There, he studied medicine.

In 1791, William's father died. William was sad because they had been close. By law, most of Benjamin's money and land went to his oldest son. William had to get a job.

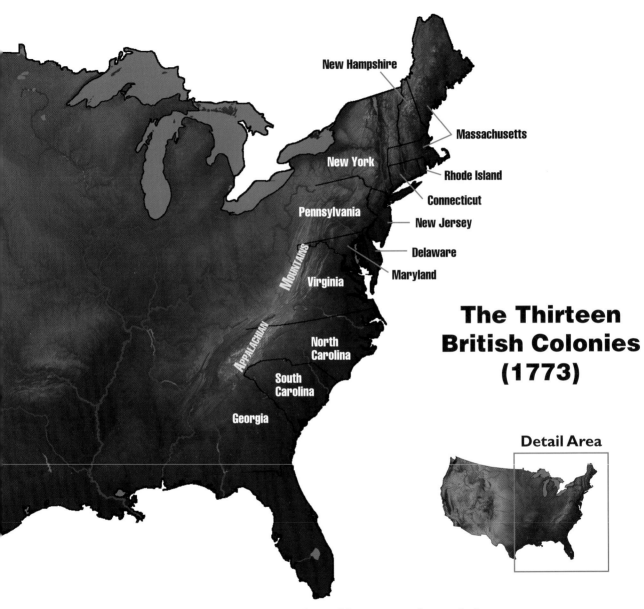

New Hampshire

Massachusetts

New York

Rhode Island

Connecticut

Pennsylvania

New Jersey

Delaware

Maryland

Virginia

North Carolina

South Carolina

Georgia

MOUNTAINS

APPALACHIAN

The Thirteen British Colonies (1773)

Detail Area

The Appalachian Mountains formed the western limits of the British colonies.

The Frontier

*H*arrison left his medical studies. He joined the military in 1791 as an **ensign**.

Harrison gathered 80 men. They marched through the Allegheny Mountains to Fort Pitt. Then they took boats down the Ohio River to Fort Washington. This new area was called the Northwest Territory. It became home to Harrison for most of his life.

Harrison learned all he could about the military. On August 20, 1794, he earned respect with his brave fighting at the Battle of Fallen Timbers. There, the U.S. Army defeated Native Americans. The battle ended all fighting in the Northwest Territory. After the battle, Harrison became a **lieutenant**.

The next year, Harrison signed the Treaty of Greenville. Native Americans gave up claims to much land.

The United States (1794)

New Hampshire

Vermont

Massachusetts

New York

Rhode Island

Pennsylvania

Connecticut

FORT PITT

New Jersey

Spanish Territory

Northwest Territory

FORT WASHINGTON

Delaware

Battle of Fallen Timbers

Maryland

Ohio River

Virginia

North Carolina

Southwest Territory

South Carolina

Georgia

Land Claimed by Spain and the U.S.

After the treaty was signed, Harrison served as commander of Fort Washington. In 1795, Harrison met and married Anna Symmes.

Family and Career

William and Anna had a long and happy marriage. The Harrisons had six sons and four daughters. The family never had a lot of money. But they were close and loving.

In 1797, Harrison became a **captain**. He quit in 1798 to settle on a farm with his family. They lived in a four-room log cabin. Over the years, Harrison added 12 more rooms.

It cost a lot of money to feed his family. But Harrison still invited many friends, strangers, and politicians home for dinner. Sometimes the family went through a whole ham in one day. The cost of feeding everyone used most of the Harrisons' money.

Harrison enjoyed farming. But to support his family, he needed more money. In June 1798, President John Adams made him secretary of the Northwest Territory. In 1799, Harrison became the Northwest Territory's first congressman.

Harrison worked hard for Americans. He pushed **Congress** for the Land Act of 1800. This law made it easier for new **settlers** to buy land. Before this law, only rich people could afford land. People liked Harrison's ideas.

President John Adams

The Making of the Ninth United States President

1773
Born February 9, Charles City County, Virginia

1787
Enters Hampden-Sydney College

1790
Leaves college to study medicine

1791
Father dies; William joins the army

1798
Leaves army to farm; becomes secretary of Northwest Territory

1799
Appointed first delegate to Congress from the Northwest Territory

1800
Appointed first governor of the Indiana Territory

1811
Harrison and U.S. troops defeat the Native Americans at Tippecanoe River

1816
Becomes a representative of Congress for Ohio

1819
Elected to the Ohio State Senate

1824
Elected to the United States Senate

1828
Serves as minister to Colombia

William H. Harrison

"The only legitimate right to govern is an expressed grant of power from the governed."

1794
Becomes a lieutenant; fights Battle of Fallen Timbers

1795
Marries Anna Symmes

1797
Becomes a captain

Historic Events
during Harrison's lifetime

★ Rosetta stone found near Rosetta, Egypt

★ Michigan becomes a state

★ *The Last of the Mohicans* published by James Fenimore Cooper

1812
Made brigadier general in the War of 1812

1813
Becomes major general; fights Battle of the Thames

1814
Leaves the army and returns home to farm

1836
Runs for president, loses to Van Buren

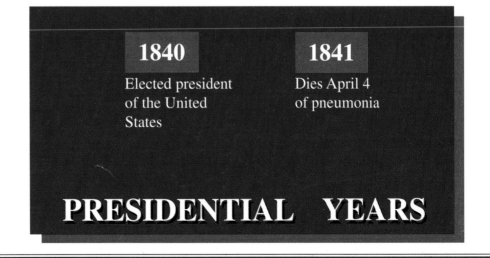

1840
Elected president of the United States

1841
Dies April 4 of pneumonia

PRESIDENTIAL YEARS

Governor Harrison

*I*n 1800, the Northwest Territory was divided into the Ohio and Indiana Territories. President Adams named Harrison the first governor of the Indiana Territory.

Native Americans controlled a great deal of land in the Northwest Territory. Harrison made treaties with them. He gained much of their land for American **settlers**.

The Shawnees, a Native American tribe, were upset about losing their land. Their leader, Tecumseh, declared war against the United States. Harrison led the American troops who fought Tecumseh. They defeated him at Tippecanoe River in 1811. Harrison became known as "Old Tippecanoe."

Harrison became a **brigadier general** in the **War of 1812**. He also was in charge of all forces in the Northwest Territory. In 1813, Harrison became a **major general**.

In 1813, Harrison recaptured Detroit from the British. He chased them into Canada. On October 5, Harrison defeated the British and their Native American **allies** in the Battle of the Thames. The battle took place on the Thames River in Ontario, Canada. Tecumseh died in the battle.

With the victory, Harrison secured America's northwestern border. He also signed a peace treaty with Native Americans from Ohio.

Harrison fought important battles at the Tippecanoe and Thames Rivers.

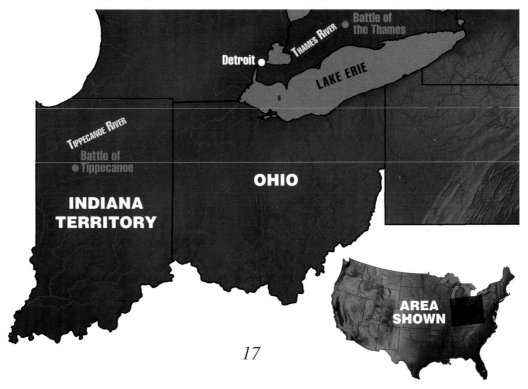

Working for His Country

*I*n 1814, Harrison quit the military. He returned to his farm. Harrison also tried his luck in other businesses. But each failed.

Harrison still wanted to work for his country. Because he was so popular in Ohio, people told him to run for **Congress**. In 1816, he became an Ohio **representative**.

Harrison ran for the Ohio state senate in 1819. He served there until 1821.

In 1824, Harrison was elected U.S. senator from Ohio. The Harrison family moved to Washington, D.C. Harrison was a senator until 1828. Then **Secretary of State** Henry Clay made him minister to Colombia.

The next year, Andrew Jackson became president. He chose a new minister to Colombia.

Many people thought Harrison could become president. He had a good record in the military and in **Congress**. Harrison ran for president in 1836. But he lost to Martin Van Buren.

Martin Van Buren

"Tippecanoe and Tyler, Too!"

*T*imes were hard in the United States in 1840. Many people were out of work. The North and the South argued about slavery. Most people blamed the problems on President Van Buren.

Harrison believed he could beat Van Buren in the next election. He chose John Tyler to be his vice president.

Harrison used new campaign ideas. He held town meetings. He had floats in parades. He gave away hats and other things to gain voter support. The campaign was like a traveling carnival. His ideas are still used today.

Harrison was shown as a military hero and a simple farmer who lived in a log cabin. The campaign used his military nickname in a song called "Tippecanoe and Tyler, Too!"

In November 1840, a record number of people voted. Harrison received the most votes. He became the ninth president of the United States.

The Battle of Tippecanoe

The Seven "Hats" of the U.S. President

A president can serve only two terms. Each term lasts four years. When Harrison was president, this law did not exist.

A president is elected or re-elected every four years.

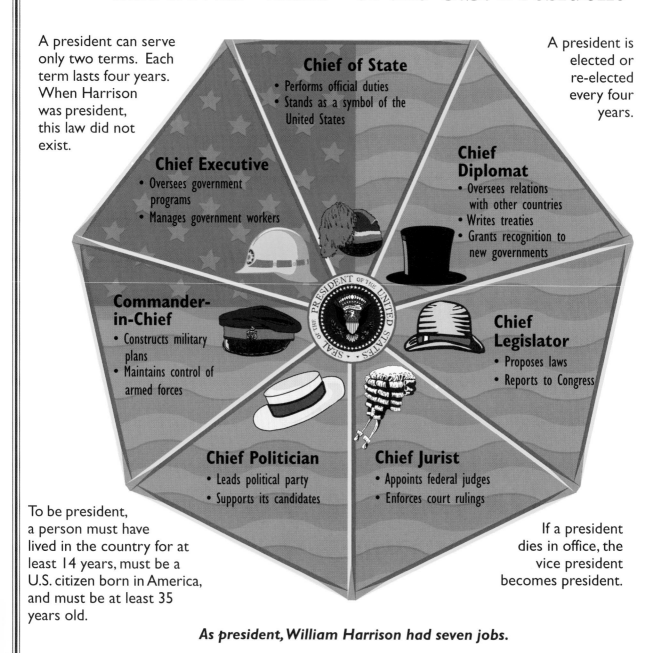

Chief of State
- Performs official duties
- Stands as a symbol of the United States

Chief Executive
- Oversees government programs
- Manages government workers

Chief Diplomat
- Oversees relations with other countries
- Writes treaties
- Grants recognition to new governments

Commander-in-Chief
- Constructs military plans
- Maintains control of armed forces

Chief Legislator
- Proposes laws
- Reports to Congress

Chief Politician
- Leads political party
- Supports its candidates

Chief Jurist
- Appoints federal judges
- Enforces court rulings

To be president, a person must have lived in the country for at least 14 years, must be a U.S. citizen born in America, and must be at least 35 years old.

If a president dies in office, the vice president becomes president.

As president, William Harrison had seven jobs.

The Three Branches of the U.S. Government

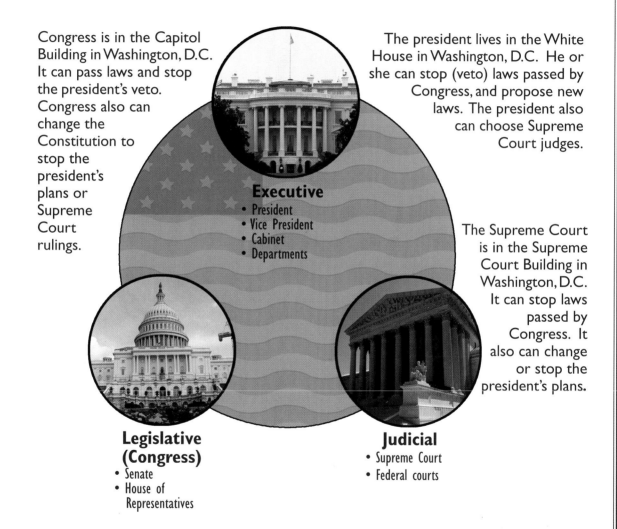

Congress is in the Capitol Building in Washington, D.C. It can pass laws and stop the president's veto. Congress also can change the Constitution to stop the president's plans or Supreme Court rulings.

The president lives in the White House in Washington, D.C. He or she can stop (veto) laws passed by Congress, and propose new laws. The president also can choose Supreme Court judges.

Executive
- President
- Vice President
- Cabinet
- Departments

The Supreme Court is in the Supreme Court Building in Washington, D.C. It can stop laws passed by Congress. It also can change or stop the president's plans.

Legislative (Congress)
- Senate
- House of Representatives

Judicial
- Supreme Court
- Federal courts

The U.S. Constitution formed three government branches. Each branch has power over the others. So, no single group or person can control the country. The Constitution calls this "separation of powers."

The Ninth President

*O*n March 4, 1841, Harrison was **inaugurated**. It was a windy, cold, and rainy day.

President Harrison gave one of the longest inaugural speeches ever. He stood in the cold rain for a long time. He did not wear a hat, coat, or gloves.

President Harrison was worn out from his long campaign. Later that month, he developed **pneumonia**.

Harrison quickly named his **cabinet**. He remained in bed until he died on April 4, 1841. It was the shortest presidency in American history.

For his wife, children, friends, and many Americans, it was a sad day. People believed Harrison could have been a great president. Though he was president for one month, he remains one of the nation's great military leaders.

Harrison rides a horse to his inauguration in 1841.

Fun Facts

- William Harrison was the only president who studied medicine. He gave it up to become a soldier.

- During the presidential campaign of 1840, Harrison's supporters rolled a huge paper ball from Kentucky to the convention in Baltimore. They shouted the slogan, "Keep the ball rolling to Washington."

- President Harrison's wife and children were not present in Washington, D.C., during his one month in office. The family planned to move there in the spring.

- When he moved into the White House, Harrison did his own marketing. He even bought a cow and helped the farmer drive it back to the White House through the streets of Washington, D.C.

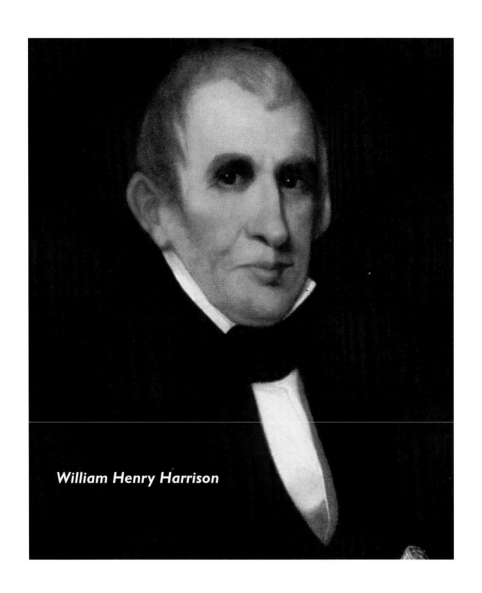

William Henry Harrison

- William Harrison's third son, John Scott Harrison, became a congressman in the 1850s. Benjamin, one of John Scott's children, became the twenty-third president of the United States.

- Harrison was not born in the United States. His birthplace, Virginia, was one of the original 13 British Colonies.

- Harrison was the first professional soldier to become president.

Opposite page:
William Harrison's grandson,
Benjamin Harrison, became
the twenty-third president.

Glossary

allies - countries that agree to help each other in times of need.

brigadier general - a one-star general.

cabinet - a group of advisers chosen by the president.

captain - a military rank above lieutenant and below major.

Congress - the lawmaking body of the U.S. It is made up of the Senate and the House of Representatives.

Declaration of Independence - a paper saying that the American colonies were free and would start their own government.

ensign - the lowest ranking officer in the military system of the 1800s.

inauguration - when a person is sworn into a political office.

lieutenant - a military rank above sergeant and below captain.

major general - a two-star general.

plantation - a large farm that grows things like cotton, tobacco, or sugar cane.

pneumonia - a disease that affects the lungs and causes high fever.

representative - a person who is elected by the people to represent a certain area. Representatives go to Washington, D.C., make laws, and are part of the House of Representatives.

secretary of state - a member of the president's cabinet who handles problems with other countries.

settlers - people who move to a new land where no one has lived before and build a community.

War of 1812 - a war fought between America and Great Britain over shipping and sailors' rights.

Internet Sites

United States Presidents Information Page
http://historyoftheworld.com/soquel/prez.htm
Links to information about United States presidents. This site is very informative, with biographies on every president as well as speeches and debates, and other links.

The Presidents of the United States of America
http://www.whitehouse.gov/WH/glimpse/presidents/html/presidents.html
This site is from the White House. With an introduction from President Bill Clinton and biographies that include each president's inaugural address, this site is excellent. Get information on White House history, art in the White House, first ladies, first families, and much more.

POTUS—Presidents of the United States
http://www.ipl.org/ref/POTUS/
In this resource you will find background information, election results, cabinet members, presidency highlights, and some odd facts on each of the presidents. Links to biographies, historical documents, audio and video files, and other presidential sites are also included to enrich this site.

These sites are subject to change. Go to your favorite search engine and type in United States presidents for more sites.

Pass It On

History enthusiasts: educate readers around the country by passing on information you've learned about presidents or other important people who have changed history. Share your little-known facts and interesting stories. We want to hear from you!

To get posted on the ABDO Publishing Company Web site, email us at "History@abdopub.com"
Visit the ABDO Publishing Company Web site at www.abdopub.com

Index

DATE DUE

MAY 3 0 2000	
NOV 1 4 2000	

BRODART, CO. Cat. No. 23-221-003